THE FAMILY COURT SURVIVAL GUIDE

Navigating the New York Family Court System

Jeffrey W. Johnson, Esq.

Jacobs & Whitehall
21750 Hardy Oak Blvd
Suite 104
#51700
San Antonio, Texas 78258
www.jacobsandwhitehall.com

Ordering Information:

Quantity sales. Special discounts are available on quantity purchases by corporations, associations, and others. For details, contact the publisher at the address above.

Orders by U.S. trade bookstores and wholesalers. Please contact Jacobs & Whitehall: Tel: (888) 991-2766 or visit www.jacobsandwhitehall.com.

Printed in the United States of America

Published in 2021

PREFACE

I graduated from Columbia Law School in 1991. I was the first in my family to go to law school, and to go to an Ivy League school. My dad was a blue collar guy, who could build or fix anything with his hands, two things I could never do. My mom was smart as a whip, but she took care of the kids and house, because that's what women did back then. They both went through the War and the Depression, lost everything, and had to start over. So I was the first to get those opportunities.

Most, not all, of my classmates at Columbia went off to make buckets of money at corporate law firms. I took a different tack (not that there's anything wrong with making buckets of money). I wanted to help people, especially people of modest means like my parents. I went to the Legal Aid Society after graduation, an organization that represents lower income people. After seven years, I opened my own practice. I still spend a lot of my time representing lower income folks, mainly parents and children in Family Court.

This "Family Court Survival Guide" is designed to help people who find themselves in Family Court. It has answers to many of the most common questions people have. Many people are worried or afraid when they're in front of a Family Court judge. What's going to happen to me? What's going to happen to my kids? Many of the answers are in here. I hope that you find it useful, that it takes some of the fear and stress away, and that it helps you and your family.

DEDICATION

I know it's not very original, but I dedicate this book to my family. My dad, the best guy I knew, who worked hard for his family, and died young, when I was 19, before he could enjoy his retirement. My mom, Mema, who kept the family together when he died, and to whom I owe everything I have, who almost made 90 last year. My wife, Ro, who tells me every day that I'm the best person she's ever known, and I saved her, but really she saved me. My son, Evan, who's a brilliant soul, officially a man now, but will always be my boy. My daughter, Lindsey, Daddy's little girl, my fiercest defender and sunset companion. Without you guys I'd be a lonely old man. I love all of you more than the sun, moon, star and skies.

DISCLAIMER

This publication is intended to be used for educational purposes only. No legal advice is being given, and no attorney-client relationship is intended to be created by reading this material. The author assumes no liability for any errors or omissions or for how this book or its contents are used or interpreted, or for any consequences resulting directly or indirectly from the use of this book. For legal or any other advice, please consult an experienced attorney or the appropriate expert, who is aware of the specific facts of your case and is knowledgeable in the law in your jurisdiction.

Law Office of Jeffrey W. Johnson
36 Richmond Terrace
Suite 202
Staten Island, NY 10301
(718) 557-9767
WWW.JeffreyWJohnsonLaw.Com

TESTIMONIALS

"Mr. Johnson was a law guardian many years ago when he was assigned to my twin sons who were at a fragile age of 6. I was going through a bitter divorce in which my ex-husband was being very cooperative with issues involving the children. Mr. Johnson was a big help in my boys being able to speak their feelings to Mr. Johnson with complete ease & confidentiality. They were hesitant at first but then gained his trust. Mr. Johnson was completely dedicated to hearing their voice and was totally dedicated to their wellbeing. I would highly recommend him."

– Kelly S.

****

"Jeffrey Johnson acted on my behalf. He listened to my concerns and addressed each one. He took the time necessary to review my case, gave me multiple options. I am very satisfied with my representation in family court. My ex-wife is difficult to say the least, Mr. Johnson made me feel confident I have a fighting chance in court."

– Michael

****

Mr. Johnson was well qualified and I appreciate all he did for me. He is excellent at his job. He answered all my questions and was always there for me. I would recommend him to anybody and would definitely use him again."

– Rosemarie

****

"Mr. Johnson answered the call from court immediately. He contacted me, made me feel comfortable. I had never met him before, He took the time to learn about details of my case. Thorough, professional, He made me feel confident going to court, prepared. I cannot thank Jeffrey Johnson enough."

– Michael N.

****

"I have known Jeff as a lawyer for 10 years. He is smart, caring and dedicated to his clients. I highly recommend him."

– Jesse E.

****

"Jeff is a caring and contentious attorney."

– Krystle B.

****

TABLE OF CONTENTS

About The Author

In 1991, I received my law degree from Colombia Law School, and began working for the Legal Aid Society until 1998. During this time, I didn't handle many family law cases. In 1998, I ventured out on my own and started handling some family law cases, and various other kinds of cases.

In 2001, I joined the New York State Family Court Assigned Counsel Panel, which is a panel comprised of lawyers who do two things: represent adults who can't afford their own attorney in Family Court, and represent children in Family Court cases involving neglect, custody, visitation, orders of protection, and child support. For the past 20 years, I've spent most of my time handling these types of family law cases, as well as some juvenile delinquency and termination of parental rights cases.

Why Write A Book?

Many people get dragged to Family Court either because a case was filed against them by the government, or because a private person filed a case against them for an order of protection, custody, child support, or visitation of a child.

Most people don't really know much about Family Court—like what function it serves, which procedures to follow, how long a case will take, what will happen to their children, and what to expect overall.

This book is designed to provide people with an understanding of the basics of family court so that they can handle their case with greater confidence in and knowledge of the process.

CHAPTER 1

NEW YORK STATE FAMILY COURT VS. SUPREME COURT

When most people think of family law, they think of divorce cases. In New York, the Supreme Court—which is the general jurisdiction court—is the only court that can handle actual divorce cases. The Supreme Court is difficult and expensive for people to navigate; there are many procedures, lots of paperwork, and a $210 filing fee (at minimum). In addition, a request for judicial intervention must be filed in order to get a judge assigned to a case, which costs another couple hundred dollars.

As a result, the New York legislature developed the Family Court as a more user-friendly alternative; it was designed to be navigated without the help of a lawyer (although it is usually beneficial to hire a lawyer anyway), as there is less paperwork, no filing fees, and it offers an overall streamlined process.

Unlike the Supreme Court, which is a general court that handles all types of cases (e.g., personal injury, criminal, business disputes, matrimonial), Family Court is a specialized court of limited jurisdiction, meaning that only particular kinds of cases can be filed in Family Court. Family Court is tailored for families who are in crisis, but cannot grant parties a divorce, nor handle equitable distribution matters (i.e., the division of property and assets).

The Family Court does have the authority to handle custody, visitation, orders of protection, paternity, and child support issues between parties who are not married, or who are married but do not have a pending divorce case. If the parties are married and are getting a divorce, then these cases would be filed in the Supreme Court in conjunction with the divorce.

Most final divorce judgments dictate that Family Court and the Supreme Court have concurrent jurisdiction over changes to custody, visitation, child support or spousal support. This means that if one party wants to increase or reduce child support, or enforce a child support order after they have already received a divorce judgment, or change or enforce custody or visitation, they would take those actions to either the Family Court or the Supreme Court (most people go through the Family Court for these matters).

Family Court can handle cases that aren't typically handled by the Supreme Court, including child protective cases involving parents who have been accused of child abuse or neglect. In New York, these cases are filed by the Administration for Children's Services (ACS) against the parents or caregivers who are legally responsible for the child;

any court case that arises from neglect or abuse would be dealt with only by the Family Court.

Family Court also handles juvenile delinquency cases, which are criminal cases involving a minor who is under the age of 18 (in the past, it was under the age of 16). Once a person turns 18 years old, they are considered an adult and can be charged as one in Criminal Court; if they are charged with a felony, then the case would be held in the Supreme Court.

There is dual jurisdiction for adoption cases, as they are handled by the Family Court as well as the New York Surrogate's Court, which is a division of the Supreme Court that handles estates, trusts, and guardianships.

If an order of protection is needed between parties who are not married, one can be sought in Family Court. In the past, an individual could only file for an order of protection through the Family Court if it was against someone with whom they were related by blood or marriage, or had a child with. The legislature has expanded the jurisdiction to allow an individual to file for an order or protection through the Family Court against someone they are in an "intimate relationship" with, which could mean they are dating, or even against a friend.

About 10 years ago, the Integrated Domestic Violence (IDV) Court was established. The IDV is a part of the Supreme Court that handles cases that are scattered in different courts. For example, one incident can lead to both an order of protection case in Family Court, and a simultaneous criminal case. There might also be a divorce case going on in the Supreme Court. The legislature established IDV Court as a way of having associated cases involving the same parties be heard by one judge.

It is not uncommon for there to be an overlap between the Family Court and Supreme Court. For instance, this would happen if one party files for custody, visitation, an order of protection, or child support in Family Court, and the other party (or even the same party) files for divorce in the Supreme Court. Under these circumstances, one person would make a motion to consolidate the cases into the divorce case, which would likely be granted for custody and visitation matters.

Since orders of protection are considered priority cases and must be decided prior to matters of custody and visitation, they will often stay in the Family Court; the same is true for child support cases.

CHAPTER 2

SPOUSAL SUPPORT AND CHILD SUPPORT

Typically, the custodial parent (i.e., the parent who has the child for the majority of the time) will be the person filing for child support against the other legal parent. However, there may be a question as to the identity of the other legal parent.

When a child is born in New York, the father will usually file an acknowledgment of paternity and his name will be on the birth certificate. If that doesn't happen, then the mother would have to establish paternity prior to filing for child support. To do so, she would file a paternity petition. A father can also file for paternity.

Paternity can be agreed to between the parties, or either party can request a DNA test to prove paternity. When paternity must be established for the purposes of obtaining a child support order, the paternity case will be converted to a child support case, and then child support would be determined.

In New York, child support is determined using a mathematical formula based on the number of children that the parties have in common. The FICA tax (i.e., Social Security and Medicare tax) and New York City income tax are subtracted from the non-custodial parent's income, and a percentage of the remaining income would be allocated to child support.

Several other expenses are considered in the determination of child support, including child care expenses, unreimbursed medical expenses, and educational expenses. These expenses are divided pro rata (i.e., according to the income of the two parents), which means that if one parent has twice as much income as the other parent, then that parent will be responsible for two-thirds of the expenses.

Spousal support is also determined using a mathematical formula based on the incomes of the two parents, as well as a consideration of which parent is paying child support.

Child Support Order Modifications

Either parent can file a petition for a modification of a child support order. Typically, the custodial parent will file a petition for upward modification, and the non-custodial parent for downward modification.

Once three years have passed since the child support order was entered, a request for modification can be filed. If three years have not passed, then the parent who files for modification must show that there has been a change of circumstances since the order was entered. For example, if the parent who is paying child support has lost their job, received a pay cut, become disabled, or otherwise lost income, then they could file for a downward modification of child support.

The parent requesting a downward modification would have to show that the decrease in income occurred through no fault of their own, and that they have been making efforts to obtain a new job (or another source of income). The party would have to complete a financial disclosure affidavit showing their expenses, debts, and income; the other party would have a chance to dispute this.

These cases are typically handled by support magistrates rather than judges. The support magistrate would hear all of the facts and make a determination as to whether the child support amount should be reduced.

The parent who is receiving child support can file for an upward modification of child support so long as they can show that the paying parent's income has increased. Obtaining an upward modification tends to be a bit easier than obtaining a downward modification because there are costs of living increases that sometimes automatically kick in.

It's not always easy to obtain a child support modification, and it helps to have the assistance of a lawyer.

CHAPTER 3

CUSTODY AND PARENTING TIME ARRANGEMENTS

When it comes to the determination of custody and parenting time arrangements in New York, the guiding principle is always the best interest of the child, which is a nebulous standard. The court has to consider all relevant aspects of the case, such as which parent has been the primary caregiver for the child, the housing situation of each parent, the desires of the child, reports and recommendations made by the attorney for the child or psychologists, whether there has been a history of ACS involvement, whether either parent has a criminal history, and whether there has been domestic violence between the parents.

The court will have to consider all of these factors and make a decision as to the best interest of the child. There is no hard-and-fast rule when it comes to the best interest standard, so it is very useful to have an attorney who has handled many of these cases and knows how to advocate for his or her client regarding the best interest of the child.

When a divorce is filed, it is typical for one parent to have the child living with them. Often, that arrangement is kept in place while the divorce is pending, but either parent can make a motion to change that situation.

If the court can justify it, they may request forensic reports by a court-appointed psychologist or social worker. This psychologist or social worker will interview the parties, including the children, and review all relevant education and medical records in order to make a recommendation to the court regarding custody and visitation.

Sole Vs. Joint Legal Custody

In New York, there are two types of custody. The first is sole custody, which is when one parent makes major decisions regarding the health, education, and welfare of the child. The other parent must be kept informed and advised of all those matters, given access to medical records, school records, etc., and be able to speak to providers.

There is also joint legal custody, which is when both parents must agree on all decisions regarding the health, education, and welfare of the child. Often, when people refer to "joint custody," what they really mean is a fifty-fifty split of time with the child, which is joint physical custody.

If one parent wants sole legal custody and the other parent wants joint legal custody, the attorneys will often work out a joint legal custody arrangement with one parent being granted final decision-making authority. This means that the parents must try to reach agreement regarding major issues involving the child, like what school they will attend, what religion they will be taught, and what medical procedures they will undergo. However, if the parents cannot reach an agreement on one or more of these issues, then the parent who has been granted final decision-making authority will have the final say.

Parenting Time Schedules

In most cases, the parents will come to an agreement regarding a parenting time schedule. If the parents cannot reach an agreement, then the court will have to make a temporary determination regarding parenting time. Typically, there won't be an order of custody while the divorce is pending unless there is a good reason for it (e.g., education-based or medical reasons). In some cases, the court will grant a temporary order of custody to the parent who's been the main caregiver.

There is a near infinite number of parenting time arrangements that can be established; it depends on the status quo at the time, the attorney for the child's recommendation, and the judge's opinion as to what is in the best interest of the child.

The typical arrangement in New York is when one parent has physical custody of the child (i.e., has the child with them for the majority of the time), and the other parent has the child with them on alternating weekends, usually overnights, and potentially a day during the week. Under this arrangement, school breaks, vacations, and holidays are split fifty-fifty between the parents.

CHAPTER 4

AVOIDING COURT INTERVENTION

Parents can agree to any type of agreement they choose without court intervention—and most attorneys will encourage parties to do this rather than accept a court-imposed order. However, such an agreement would not be enforceable unless it's a written stipulation signed by the parties and ordered by the court, or an order of the court. In other words, an oral agreement between parents would not be enforceable. That said, an oral agreement would carry some weight should one parent eventually deviate or wish to deviate from that agreement, as it would stand as the status quo.

The Child's Voice

The child is always allowed to provide input as to which parent they would like to live with or spend the majority of their time with, although this input is never determinative; the guiding principle on such decisions is always the best interest of the child.

There will almost always be an attorney for the child assigned to the case, and that attorney will interview the child. Depending on the age of the child, the attorney will either advocate for what they think is in the best interest of the child or for what the child wants. In New York, once a child is six years old, the attorney for the child is bound to treat them as any other client and to advocate for what they want.

The older the child is, the more weight their wishes will carry. The court is not going to tell a 17-year-old child that they must live with their mother if they have clearly expressed that they would like to live with their father; such an order would be very difficult to enforce without evidence that the father is totally unfit to care for the child.

Calling On Specialists

If either parent raises an issue regarding child endangerment, neglect, or abuse by the other parent, then the court will order an investigation by ACS. Such situations could involve a number of allegations, including drug use or poor living conditions. An ACS case worker will investigate the claims made, which will typically involve interviewing the parents and the child, investigating the homes of each parent, and determining whether either parent has a criminal history or there has been a history of ACS involvement. Based on this information, ACS will issue a report to the court that states whether they believe there is any danger to the child. An ACS investigation of this sort could occur at any point during a case.

When parents cannot agree on custody and visitation matters, and/or when certain issues exist in a case, the court may order forensic reports, which will be completed by a psychologist, psychiatrist, or social worker. The chosen professional will interview the parents, the child, and anyone else who they believe could provide useful information about the situation. They will also review medical and education records. Ultimately, the professional will write a detailed report containing custody and visitation recommendations to the court. Typically, the court will appoint the professional to create forensic reports, but the parents may have to pay $2,500 or more upfront for their services.

Modifications To Custody And Parenting Time Agreements

Either parent can file for a modification to the custody or parenting time agreement at any time. To do so, they must show that there has been a fairly significant change in circumstances, such as relocation by one parent, or a change in the child's needs or desires which impacts the custody or visitation agreement.

If the parties don't agree that there's been a change in circumstances, then the court can hold a change of circumstances hearing. If the court finds that there has been a change in circumstances, then the court must determine whether a modification to the existing custody or visitation order is in the child's best interest.

Guardianship In New York State

In New York State, guardianship and custody are essentially synonymous. If someone has guardianship over a child, they make the major decisions regarding the health, education, and welfare of the child. If a nonparent is filing (e.g., sibling, aunt, uncle, or individual with no familial relation to the child), then the court will treat it as a guardianship petition; if a parent or grandparent is filing, then the court will treat it as a custody petition.

In practice, the only major difference between guardianship and custody is that guardianship of a child holds until the age of 21 and custody of a child holds until the age of 18. Aside from that, the standards regarding who receives guardianship or custody are basically the same.

If a nonparent wins guardianship of a child, then they will have the authority to make decisions regarding the child's health, education, and welfare. This, however, does not mean that the parent's parental rights are terminated; the parent would still have legal rights to visitation and child support obligations.

In addition, an award of guardianship to a nonparent is not necessarily permanent, as the parent can attempt to regain custody of the child. To accomplish this, the parent would have to show that there's been a change in circumstances, and that it would be in the child's best interest for custody to be transferred back to them.

CHAPTER 5

ORDERS OF PROTECTION

In New York, an order of protection from a court prohibits a person from taking certain actions related to another person.

A "usual terms" order of protection lists a number of such actions, including assault, menacing, harassment, threats, disorderly conduct, and various sexual offenses. A full stay away order typically prohibits a person from contacting another person in any way, including by phone, email, social media, and via a third party. The person is also prohibited from going near the other person's home, school, or place of business.

If a person files for an order of protection against someone with whom they have a familial or intimate relationship or share a child, then they can seek an order of protection through Family Court. A Criminal or Supreme Court can issue an order of protection on behalf of the victim of an assault in a criminal case.

In a Family Court case, a temporary order of protection is typically renewed at each court date. A final order of protection can last anywhere from one day to two years, though under normal circumstances, they usually last one to two years. Under extraordinary circumstances, such as those involving a weapon, an order of protection can last for five years in Family Court. In Criminal Court, orders of protection typically last for several years, but it depends on the severity of the crime.

A Family Court judge will often issue an order of protection against a parent who is accused of neglect or abuse. Typically, this type of order would either prohibit the parent from contacting their child, or allow only court-sanctioned visitation. If the party in such a case is not a parent of the child, then there would likely be a final order of protection prohibiting the party from contacting the child until the child is 18 years of age.

Due to a development over the past few years, a person can file a petition to extend an order of protection in Family Court. This means that if a one-year order of protection was granted and the individual wants it to last longer, they can file for an extension prior to the end of that one-year period.

Violation of an order of protection is a felony in New York State, punishable by a maximum sentence of seven years in prison. In response to a violation of a Family Court order of protection, in addition to calling the police, an individual can file a violation petition in Family Court. If it is determined that the other party intentionally violated the Family Court order of protection, they can be held in contempt of court, which is punishable by a maximum of six months in prison.

In the end, an order of protection is just a piece of paper, so it certainly doesn't prevent someone from doing harm to another person. That said, it does offer a layer of protection beyond the law itself, because it can result in a person being incarcerated based on any violation of the order.

Responding To An Order Of Protection

In response to an order of protection, a person has several options, one of which is to do nothing. This would be an option if the person has no intention of ever being around the person again. They would need to be careful not to violate the order or protection, or else they could be arrested or subject to contempt in Family Court.

If an order of protection is taken out between family members or people who have a child together, then the individual would certainly want to answer the order of protection by appearing in court and either consenting to or fighting the order of protection. People who consent usually do so without admitting any wrongdoing, and the two parties would agree on a period of time during which the order would be valid.

If the parties have a child together and the order of protection includes a stay away order that applies to the child, then the individual may want to fight the order of protection. When children are involved, these situations can become complicated, and it may be wise to hire an attorney who can negotiate for the child to not be included in the order of protection. Some orders of protection will say that they are subject to future Family Court or Supreme Court orders which would allow the parent to file for visitation with the child.

CHAPTER 6

CHILD PROTECTIVE CASES

A child protective (CP) case in New York is filed by the Administration for Children's Services (ACS). Once someone makes a report to the confidential child abuse hotline through the Central Registry of Child Abuse and Neglect, ACS will launch an investigation into the allegations.

If ACS cannot confirm the allegations, then they will close the case file; if they confirm the allegations, then they will request that the offending parent cooperate with ACS home visits, drug testing, classes, or other requirements. If the case is too serious for this course of action, then ACS will file an abuse or neglect petition in Family Court. ACS may ask for a remand of the children, which means they will try to remove the children from the parent(s) accused of neglect. Alternatively, ACS will consent to the children remaining with the parents under certain conditions.

When I am retained on a private CP case, I generally represent one of the parents or the persons legally responsible for the children (it could be a nonparent, boyfriend, girlfriend, relative, or anyone else who is accused of neglect). If parents prove that they are financially eligible, I may be assigned to represent them in Family Court. In some cases, I will be assigned as an attorney for the child.

Common CP Cases

The most common allegations which prompt a CP case or ACS investigation have to do with drugs, including anything from prescription drugs to alcohol. In some cases, a parent is accused of being under the influence while caring for their child, or driving under the influence with their child in the car. In other cases, a child will test positive for drugs or alcohol at birth. In these and similar situations, ACS will file a case against the parents, and if the issue is serious enough, seek to remove the child from the parents.

Excessive corporal punishment is a common reason for the initiation of an ACS investigation or CP case. While it is legal to use corporal punishment or physical punishment against a child in New York, it is not legal to use excessive corporal punishment, often evidenced by the use of an implement (e.g., belt) and marks left on the child.

Another common reason for a CP case is abandonment, which is said to occur when a child of insufficient age is left alone for a period of time in a house or vehicle. If ACS finds an abandonment issue, they will often remove the child from the house.

Other bases for CP cases include poor or inadequate living conditions (e.g., a very dirty house), medical neglect whereby the parent is failing to meet the child's medical or psychiatric needs, and educational neglect marked by excessive absence from school.

The Process Of An ACS Investigation

ACS will launch an investigation into any allegation of child abuse or neglect. If ACS substantiates the allegation, then they will put in services or supervision over the family; if the case is more serious in nature, then they will file a case in the Family Court.

These cases can follow one of two paths. The first possibility is that ACS will decide not to remove the child from the home, but will impose safeguards (e.g., drug testing, home visits, an order of protection prohibiting the parents from certain actions). The second possibility is that ACS will decide to remove the child from the home, either by exercising their emergency power to do so, or by asking the court to approve removal of the child.

The parent has the right to request a hearing in front of a Family Court judge to prevent a removal or to request the return of a child who has already been removed. At that hearing, ACS must prove that there's imminent risk to the life, health, or safety of the child, while the parent—through their attorney, typically—

would need to show that there is no imminent risk to the life, health, or safety of the child. This hearing is considered an emergency hearing, which means it must be held on the day that ACS plans to remove the child, or if the child has already been removed, then within three days of that removal.

After the hearing, the judge will determine whether they believe ACS has met their burden of proving imminent risk to the child. If they find that ACS has proven that, then the judge will authorize ACS to remove the child; if they find that ACS has failed to meet their burden of proof, then they will prevent the removal of the child, or have the child returned to the parent.

Typically, a case will be adjourned for settlement conferences, where ACS will have to turn over all their evidence to the attorneys for the parents. The attorney for the child (who, in most cases, is from the Legal Aid Society) will meet with the child, and depending on their age, advocate for what the child wants, or for what they believe is in the best interest of the child.

The process might involve several court appearances. At some point, the case may be resolved through a negotiated settlement between the parents' attorneys, the ACS attorney, and the attorney for the child; alternatively, there will be a trial.

If a case goes to trial, the first stage would be the fact-finding stage, where ACS would have to prove by "a preponderance of the evidence" that neglect or abuse has been committed by the parent or person who is legally responsible for the child. The "preponderance of the evidence" standard is not as difficult to meet as the "beyond a reasonable doubt" standard, since all that must be shown is that there is more evidence to support one side of the case as opposed to the other.

If ACS proves their case, then disposition will follow, which is when the judge decides what will happen with the child and parents. The judge may decide to remove or maintain ACS custody of the child, which would typically mean that the child would remain in or be placed in foster care or a family member's home. Alternatively, the judge may order ACS supervision for a period of time, during which the child would stay with the parents, but the parents would have to comply with certain services (e.g., parenting classes, drug treatment). If the parents comply for a certain period of time, then the supervision would end and the ACS case would be closed.

If the child is placed in foster care, there must be a permanency hearing held every six months. At this hearing, the court will monitor the situation with the parents and the child, and check to see whether the parents are visiting their child, cooperating with ACS, and otherwise working toward regaining custody of their child.

If the child is not returned to the parents in a timely manner, which is usually determined by the child being in foster care for 15 out of 22 months, then the foster care agency may be required to start a termination of parental rights case. If parental rights are terminated, it is typically because it is alleged that the parents have failed to cooperate with the services and do what is necessary to regain custody of their child. Once parental rights have been terminated, the child could be adopted.

Outcome Of Abuse And Neglect Cases

In the best case scenario, a child neglect or abuse case will get dismissed. Typically, this would only happen after a trial. If ACS cannot prove a case or if the parent has improved to the point that ACS does not feel court intervention is necessary, then ACS may choose to withdraw their case (this does not happen often).

Most abuse and neglect cases end up getting resolved by what's called a 1051A, which is a section of the New York Family Court Act. Through this type of resolution, the party will consent to a finding of neglect against them without admitting that they did anything wrong. Alternatively, the case could be resolved by an adjournment contemplating dismissal (ACD), which is when there is no finding of neglect against the parent and the case is typically held in abeyance for anywhere from a couple of months to a year. If the parent does everything they're supposed to do, then the case will be dismissed and sealed.

If a neglect or abuse case goes to trial and the parent loses, or if they consent to a finding of neglect or abuse, then the child could be placed in foster care.

At that point, it would be very important for the parent to cooperate with the services in order to have their child returned to them. This might mean completing drug treatment, taking drug tests, visiting regularly with the child, and having adequate housing and income to care for the child.

It can be very difficult for a person to accomplish all of this on their own, which is why it is best to hire a lawyer. Low-income individuals may be able to have an attorney appointed to them. It is very important for parents to have someone who is familiar with the Family Court and child protective cases, and who can advocate for them during negotiations, hearings, and trials.

CHAPTER 7

THE IMPORTANCE OF AN EXPERIENCED FAMILY LAW ATTORNEY

Most family law cases are difficult to navigate without the help of an attorney. The exceptions are very simple cases, such as a paternity case where both parents agree to paternity and do not need a DNA test—only an order of paternity. That said, even if a lawyer is needed, parents may have to forgo one if they cannot afford to hire one and are not eligible to have one assigned to them, or are not entitled to an attorney.

For those who can afford to hire a lawyer, it is highly advisable to do so, especially if they have a custody or visitation, order of protection, neglect, or parental rights case. It can be extremely beneficial to have an attorney who knows all the intricacies of Family Court, knows how to examine the evidence and object to it when necessary, and can provide representation during hearings, negotiations, or trial.

A good attorney will know the parameters of a "good" settlement, because they will have years of experience negotiating for them. The outcome of a family law matter is almost always better when a lawyer is involved.

The Law Office Of Jeffrey W. Johnson

Since 2001, I have handled thousands of Family Court cases, and taken hundreds of cases to trial. I am on the assigned counsel and attorneys for children panels, and take trainings every few months in order to remain on these panels and stay current on the latest issues. For me, a typical week means being in the Family Court anywhere from two to five days.

As a result of this experience, I truly know the ins and outs of Family Court. I'm very familiar with the judges and other attorneys, as well as highly respected by them. I am well-versed in the applicable law, the possible outcomes of a case, and what can and cannot be negotiated under a particular set of circumstances. I also know how to prevent adverse outcomes at hearings and trials by knowing when a settlement as opposed to a trial should be sought. In almost every case, I am able to quickly identify the best course of action for my clients.

I make sure to be available to my clients via phone, email, and text, and always strive to provide them with the best representation regardless of the circumstances, because that's what they deserve.

My experience sets me apart from the rest—and especially from attorneys who don't spend much time in the Family Courts. Many divorce or criminal attorneys will sometimes appear in Family Court, but they really aren't familiar with the intricacies of it, and are not well known to the judges, attorneys, and staff.

INDEX

NOTES